Between the Lines
A Journey with Poetry and Reflection

Co-Created by Reverend Sam Houser and YOU

Tehom Center Publishing is a 501(c)3 nonprofit publishing feminist and queer authors, with a commitment to elevate BIPOC writers. Its face and voice is Rev. Dr. Angela Yarber.

Paperback ISBN: 978-1-966655-15-2

Ebook ISBN: 978-1-966655-16-9

Contents

For those who stayed, and those who could not, and for my beloved family, who stayed with me in creativity, reminding me that art can be both a home and a refuge. This is for you. Keep creating...

Acknowledgment

Lovies… all of my readers—your willingness to sit with these words gives them breath and meaning. To my poem-a-day writing cohort, thank you for your companionship and inspiration, for being a constant source of encouragement and accountability on this shared journey of creation. And to those who engaged with me on my socials, thank you for inspiration that crosses the universe and yet still speaks to the moment.

Author's Note

There's a rhythm to life that often gets drowned out in the noise of routine. We wake up to alarms, not to the gentle hum of the world waking with us. We move through tasks, checking off boxes, without truly inhabiting a single moment. But poetry offers a different kind of rhythm. It invites us to pause, to listen —to not just hear the words, but to feel them. And in that still-ness, we begin to see the world differently, as though through a softer, more focused lens.

You hold this book now because somewhere, deep inside, you feel that pull. That yearning for something more intentional, more present. This book is more than a collection of poems; it's an invitation to weave poetry into the fabric of your everyday life and the cycles that you are living through. Not as an escape, but as a way of entering your life more fully.

Let me ask you: When was the last time you sat still, really still, and let a moment, a word, or even just your breath move you? Poetry is a practice, not just an art form. It's a way of slowing down, of noticing, of sitting with something long enough to see it transform into meaning. This practice of reading —a single poem, or just a few lines—is a way to reconnect with that sacred rhythm you've always had but may have forgotten how to hear.

Poetry works on a different timeline than the rest of our world. It doesn't rush; it doesn't demand productivity. It asks us to be present, to feel, to sit with complexity and simplicity alike. When you read a poem, you're giving yourself permission to pause. You're carving out space to breathe. You're allowing yourself to experience beauty, pain, joy, or sorrow in bite-sized moments that nourish your spirit in ways you may not even notice at first.

Think of reading poetry like planting a seed. You read a line, a stanza, a poem, and at first, it may feel like nothing has changed. But days later, that line might return to you. It might grow inside you, changing the way you see your morning commute, or the way you listen to a loved one speak. A poem can reframe an ordinary moment, infusing it with a sense of awe.

As you are able, let yourself take a little time—whether it's with your morning coffee or right before you close your eyes at night. Whether it is a daily practice or something you turn to in the bigger moments you experience throughout life. Let these words offer you something you didn't expect: a new question, a new understanding, a feeling you couldn't quite name until the poem named it for you. Some poems might speak to you right away; others might remain quiet until the time is right. Some poems you may want to read multiple times.

In the pages that follow, you'll find poems that explore life in all its richness—the joys, the sorrows, the in-between spaces that often go unnoticed. This is your space to encounter those feelings, to reflect on them, and to allow them to spark something new in you.

But this book is only half-finished without you.

At the end of the book, there are blank pages. These are your pages. They're for you to jot down a thought, a feeling, or even your own poem. Don't overthink it. This isn't about creating something perfect; it's about showing up for yourself. Just as the poems invite you to pause and reflect, these blank spaces ask you to join the conversation.

You don't have to be a poet to write poetry. You don't have to have the "right words" to capture a moment. You simply need to listen—to yourself, to the world around you, to whatever stirs within as you read these poems. Let your pen move. Let your thoughts flow. Some days you may fill the page, others you may simply jot down a word or two. It's all part of the practice.

Guided Reflection

AT THE END OF EACH READING, TAKE A MOMENT TO REFLECT ON what has shifted for you. Did a particular poem linger in your thoughts? Did something in your week remind you of a line you read? Use the provided spaces to capture these reflections. And if a particular line or phrase sparked your own creativity, don't be afraid to underline that line. Maybe you even want to use it as a prompt to write your own poetry. There's no wrong way to do this—only the way that feels most authentic to you.

Here's a suggestion to help you get started: after reading each poem, take a few moments to sit with it. Then, answer these questions in your blank space:

- What did I feel when I read this poem? Where, in my body, am I experiencing that feeling?
- Is there a word or phrase that stood out to me?
- How does this poem reflect something in my own life?

By giving yourself the space to write and reflect, you're building a dialogue with poetry, with yourself, and with the world around you. Over time, you'll notice how these reflections become a part of your rhythm—a way to live more intentionally, more attentively, and with a deeper appreciation for the beauty found in the ordinary.

As you move through this book, know that each page is a step in your journey toward greater presence. You're not just reading poems; you're creating a sacred practice of mindfulness, creativity, and reflection. And each time you open these pages, you're making space for your soul to breathe.

This is not a race or a task to complete. It's an invitation. An invitation to slow down, to listen, and to be fully present in your life. Embrace the pauses, the silences between the words. Trust that the process is working within you, even if you can't always see it.

In this book, you'll find both the words of others and the space for your own. You'll find a practice that nourishes, that grounds, and that invites you to be wholly present in the beautiful, messy, tender moments of life.

Now, let's begin.

Part One
Chaos

The Weight We Carry

Piled like secrets in the pockets of our hearts.
They pull us low, make us bend in ways
we were never taught to straighten from.

Don't *should* on yourself—
the voice echoes like a mercy call,
like the only lifeline some days.
A reminder that maybe the load
was never really ours,
that maybe we could empty our hands
and not lose ourselves in the release.

But we carry anyway—
each weight named after someone we love,
or someone we fear,
or someone we've yet to even meet.

So, don't *should* on yourself—
don't build mountains out of other people's visions,
don't layer on another ache, another apology
for needing to breathe beneath it all.

Let the weights slip loose.
Drop them, one by one.
And watch what remains standing
when the burden finally breaks.

When Words Fail

It's in the silences, the hollow spaces between breaths,
where words used to fit like pieces in a puzzle,
that ache sharpens its edges.

I open my mouth, try to speak—
but language breaks,
cracks like old porcelain,
the words tumbling out in shards
that don't say nearly enough.

You ask me what's wrong,
and I could fill a library with the answer,
but all that spills is a sigh,
a half-smile, something unfinished.

What I mean to say is
I'm reaching for you, for anyone,
through the fog of syllables and sounds,
trying to make bridges out of splinters,
trying to name the shadow
that's been living under my skin.

What I mean to say is
I'm still here—
even when my voice isn't.

Never-ending night

As I lay me down to sleep… the world's finally quiet,
but your mind is anything but.
It's a carnival at midnight,
all bright lights and spinning wheels,
all noise where there should be silence.

The pillow feels like a question
you don't know how to answer,
the sheets a tangled mess
of unsolved riddles.

Your body is tired—so tired—
but your thoughts run marathons,
each lap faster than the last.

You count sheep, but they all have names.
Worries, regrets, plans,
all hopping the fence in your brain,
never quite landing on the other side.
You chase the idea of sleep
like it's something you've misplaced—
a set of keys, a pair of glasses—
but it slips through your fingers
like water,
like time.

And then the clock becomes your enemy,
its hands ticking too loud,
reminding you how late it is,
how long you've been awake,
how close the morning is to stealing your chance
for rest.

You stare at the ceiling
and it stares back,
a void that holds every thought
you've ever tried to forget.
You wonder if the stars are sleeping
or if they, too, are wide awake,
burning through the night
because they don't know how to stop.

And then—
the birds start singing,
the sky bleeds into dawn,
and you realize the night
has swallowed you whole.
There is no surrender,
only the weight of hours
piled up behind your eyes,
too heavy to carry,
too light to let you rest.

So you rise with the sun,
not because you're ready,
but because the world demands it,
and you walk into the day
like a shadow,
half-alive,
haunted by the sleep
that never came.

Night Folk

They come with the shroud of dusk,
the mountain air thick with stories too sharp for daylight.
Night Folk, their whispers curl like woodsmoke,
their footsteps a dance between realms—
guardians, tricksters, protectors of edges.
In shadowed forests of Switzerland,
they weave between birches and pines,
their breath the frost that bites through your scarf.
In the Black Forest of Germany,
their presence hums beneath the canopy,
warning the careless and guiding the wise.
And in the valleys of Austria,
they tread softly, where stars press low to the earth,
their songs echoing against stone.
They remind us that darkness is never empty,
but brimming with the untamed—
wild truths, forgotten lessons,
the mysteries that walk hand in hand with fear.
Stay respectful, they whisper,
when the wind steals your voice,
when the night wraps itself tightly around you.
For the Night Folk do not take,
they offer:
a chance to see yourself reflected in the quiet chaos
of all that cannot be seen.

Rhythm of Crisis

There's a pulse
to panic—
a thrum beneath your skin,
a beat too fast to hold.
You're walking
the thin wire of chaos,
one foot slipping
with every headline,
every shiver
that threads down your spine.

The clock laughs
at your racing heart,
each tick another reminder
that calm is somewhere
in the next breath,
if you can catch it.
You reach out,
hands trembling,
to find the solidness
in the mess:
a phone call,
a voice steady in the noise,
a promise
that we've survived this storm
before.

Internal Struggle

There are days
when the mind is a storm,
every thought a lightning strike
splitting open the quiet.
Your heart races
not because it's running,
but because it's trapped
between fight and flight.

You close your eyes,
try to find the off switch,
try to fold yourself
into a smaller story,
a calmer chapter.
But even then,
your breath is a broken metronome,
keeping time in a world
that doesn't wait.

So you inhale,
slow and jagged,
press your feet to the floor,
remember the earth
still holds you,
even when nothing else does.

Midnight Thoughts

It's 3 a.m.,
the hour when the world holds its breath,
when the dark feels heavy
like it's carrying secrets
no one else is willing to hold.
I'm lying here, still, as if stillness itself
might stop the gears in my head
from grinding, grinding, grinding.

This is the hour of *what ifs*,
of *should haves*,
when I start to count the things I didn't do,
the people I let slip,
the words I left unsaid,
each one a small thorn
under my skin.

There's something about midnight,
the way it peels back the layers,
shows us raw and unguarded,
whispers our fears like lullabies
meant to keep us wide awake.
You wonder if maybe, just maybe,
the stars are laughing,
watching us fold ourselves
into knots over futures
we can't even touch.

Tonight, I think of everyone I've ever loved,
the ones I can't seem to let go,
how memory turns their faces soft,
how in the quiet I almost hear their voices
like a song I forgot the words to

but hum anyway.

In this hour, the heart gets greedy,
begging for things it knows
it can't have—
closure, forgiveness, the clean edge of certainty
that morning won't grant.

And so I breathe.
Let the clock tick its way toward dawn.
Because this, too, is a kind of prayer,
the slow letting go,
the choosing to be here,
to feel the ache of everything undone
and know it's part of the story.

Tomorrow, I'll rise, hold it softer,
maybe even laugh at the things that held me captive.
But tonight, I'll let the darkness be a mirror,
reflecting all the broken, beautiful edges
of what it means to be human
and still dreaming, still reaching—
because I can't seem to stop
holding on to the light
even when it hides.

Wild Barbaras

Wild Barbaras,
they say you bloom
only in the heart of winter,
your golden petals defiant
against December's frostbitten breath.
You are a promise
whispered on Saint Barbara's Eve,
cut branches bursting into flower
while snow keeps secrets outside.
Legends weave you as stubborn joy—
the kind that grows
when no one is looking,
the kind that dares to say:
life will find a way.
Even in the dark,
even in the cold,
even when the earth seems too weary to dream.
You remind us that wild things—
Barbaras, blooms,
or people fighting storms—
are not tamed by time or frost.
They are held by the hands of hope,
rooted in centuries,
resilient as faith
that spring
will always
return.

The Mirror Lies

The mirror is a funhouse,
bending your reflection
until you can't remember
the shape you're meant to be.

Every bite feels like a battle—
your fork a weapon,
your plate an enemy,
and hunger becomes something
you're too ashamed to admit.
You starve the body
to quiet the mind,
but the silence only deepens the ache.

You lose track of yourself,
count calories like they're sins,
feel your bones push through skin
that you no longer recognize.
And still, it isn't enough.
It's never enough.

Because the mirror lies,
and you believe it
more than you believe
in your own worth.

Waiting

Time moves sideways
when crisis hits.
The seconds pull
and fold in on themselves,
holding you hostage
in their uneven rhythm.
You pace the floor,
cracking the silence
with muttered prayers,
half-hearted,
desperate.

Outside, the world
goes on as if
nothing has changed.
Birds call to each other,
leaves skitter across the pavement,
but your heartbeat
screams over it all,
waiting for a signal
to move forward
or fall apart.

When the phone rings,
you brace yourself—
knuckles white,
breath held,
ready for whatever comes.
Ready, because you must be.

Overwhelm

Some days it feels like the world is a mountain
and you are carrying it on your back.
It's the way your shoulders burn
beneath the weight of too many truths—
too many ways that injustice has carved its name
into the bones of our existence.
And every step you take
feels like another reason to give up.
The air tastes of ash and smoke,
and the sky, heavy with storms,
presses down like the hands of all those
who would rather you stay small,
stay quiet.
But you've been loud, haven't you?
You've shouted against the walls they've built,
your voice a fist
pounding on the doors of a world
that wants to keep you locked out.
Still, they tell you,
one voice can't move a mountain.
But what they don't know
is that you aren't just one voice.
You are the echo of a thousand stories—
the whispered prayers of those who came before,
the cries of all those still standing beside you.
You are carrying more than weight,
you are carrying everyone's hope
that things could be different,
could be better.
And yet the oppressions pile up.
Racism, sexism, homophobia,
poverty, violence, fear—
they stack like stones in your pockets,

dragging you down into a world
that never seems to change,
never seems to care.
It's easy to feel small in the face of it all,
like the wind could blow you away
and no one would even notice.
But here you are, still standing,
even as the storms rage on,
even as the stones press harder into your skin.
You are still here, still breathing,
and that is something.
That is everything.
Because you've learned
that the weight isn't yours alone to bear.
You've seen others,
their backs bent beneath the same burdens,
their hands outstretched toward yours.
And together,
you start to build something new—
a way to carry the heaviness
without letting it crush you.
You'll stitch a quilt of resistance
from every thread of solidarity,
and wrap it around your shoulders
like armor.
You'll find moments of rest
in the space between the battles,
and plant seeds of hope
in the cracks of this broken world.
Yes, the oppressions are many,
and the weight is real.
But so is your strength.
So is your will to rise,
again and again,
no matter how many times
they try to push you down.

You'll gather every stone they throw
and build a bridge
so others can follow,
so no one has to walk alone
beneath the burden.
And someday,
maybe not today,
maybe not tomorrow,
but someday—
the weight will shift.
The stones will fall,
and what's left behind
won't be a mountain
but a path forward,
where hope can finally run free.

Frau Perchta

She comes with winter's edge,
a silver thread of frost in her wake,
feet crunching over the brittle bones of autumn leaves.
Frau Perchta, the weaver, the keeper, the judge—
her spindle sharp enough to split truth from lie,
her presence a shadow cast by our choices.
And Frau Gaude dances behind her,
a wild laugh that echoes through the cold,
her joy not careless but careful,
like the warmth of a fire tending itself.
She knows life's feast and famine,
knows how to make revelry
from the scraps we are too proud to cherish.
Together, they walk—
guardians of the dual heart of the season.
One warns, Do your work.
The other whispers, Find your joy.
Both insist:
You are the thread and the loom,
the feast and the hunger,
the snowstorm and the thaw.
When they pass, look closely.
Your reflection lives in their wake.

Depression

Some days,
the sky feels like it's sinking,
like it's been stapled to the top of your head,
and no matter how hard you push against the air,
it doesn't lift.
Some days, you forget what light looks like,
how it feels to be kissed by the sun
instead of swallowed by shadows.

You forget that hope
used to have a voice,
a song.
Now it just hums under your skin,
barely a whisper,
like the buzzing of a dying light bulb,
flickering on the edge of going out.

There are days when the weight
isn't in your chest, but in your bones,
like you're made of stone
and someone carved a name into you,
not your own,
but something like "empty,"
something like "never enough."
And no one told you that surviving
could feel like this.

Some days,
your breath comes like a stranger
knocking at your door,
and you pretend you're not home.
Some days, you are not home.
You are lost in the house

you used to know,
every room a maze of unspoken sadness,
every window shut tight
against the cold that never leaves.

But then—
there are days when you remember.
When you stand at the edge of the cliff
and hear the ocean calling your name,
reminding you that even in the deepest blue,
there is life.
You hear it
in the way the waves refuse to stop,
in the way the tide keeps pulling itself back
even when it's tired.

Some days, you learn to be the ocean.
To keep moving,
even when it feels like you can't.
Some days, you reach for the sun,
and though it's far,
you know it's there,
waiting,
just beyond the next breath.

Anxiety's Voice

Anxiety is a room with no doors,
no windows,
just walls that creep closer,
tightening like breath
stuck in the chest.

It's the feeling of too much—
too many thoughts,
too many things you can't touch,
can't hold,
can't fix.

Your mind, a restless hum,
buzzing like a thousand bees
with nowhere to land.
Every step forward feels like a stumble,
like the ground is shifting under you
just as you find your footing.

It's the pause before the fall,
the dread of a storm that may never come
but still keeps you tethered to its shadow.

Anxiety whispers: *prepare for the worst.*
And you listen—
because how can you not?
But somewhere, deep down,
there's a voice that counters,
soft and steady: *breathe, just breathe,*
and you try,
even when it feels like too much to ask.

The Day Spills Over

It's all too much—
the stack of dishes tipping over,
the checkbook we never balanced,
the sky itself, relentless,
churning up another storm,
because it can, because it must,
because nature feels everything,
feels us.

And here we are,
arms barely holding
the pieces of ourselves we once promised
to protect—
small, trembling fragments
we polish and prop up each day,
telling ourselves it's enough.

But each morning looks like the one before,
and somehow we're on repeat,
coffee cup to dirty dish,
clock to unread book,
the space between us and yesterday
shrinking with each hour.

The days are blurring like a watercolor left in the rain—
colors bleeding, edges dissolving,
our plans ink-washed down to empty shades of intention.

We're breathing, yes,
but barely.
We're a list half-checked,
a pile of nearlys,
a thousand things we wanted to fix

but set aside
because
it was all too much.

So maybe today, we let go.
Drop one thing, or two,
watch them hit the ground—
whatever decides to stay whole
is what we'll call worthy,
is what we'll call ours.

We'll learn to live with what's left,
to love the bones of ourselves,
even if they're splintered,
even if they hold us
only because we asked them
one more time.

And in that small space,
the one we thought was loss,
something steady—
maybe peace,
maybe the kind of hope
that doesn't care
if it blurs into tomorrow

Working Bones

It's dawn, and the bones are already tired—
they creak like floorboards, old wood in the winter,
a body held together by habit, by want,
by a threadbare belief in tomorrow.

The coffee brews, black as night left behind,
and my hands hold it like something sacred,
like it might be enough
to wake more than just my eyes.

I walk into the day
like a machine with gears worn down,
like hope might be a muscle
that keeps moving anyway.

Winter is Coming

SAD is the weight of winter,
the sun slipping farther away
like it's forgotten how to rise for you.
It's the gray that hangs
heavy on your bones,
where even the air feels like too much
to carry in your lungs.

It's the morning that never quite breaks,
the endless twilight that blurs the line
between waking and sleeping,
and still,
you're tired.
You're always so tired.

The cold creeps in,
but it's more than the frost
on the windows,
it's the freeze inside your chest,
the stillness that feels like nothing can thaw.

It's the world dimming
without your permission,
like someone's pulled the plug on color
and left you in muted tones.
You forget what warmth feels like,
what joy felt like
before the dark crept in.

And yet, you wait.
Because somewhere,
maybe in the smallest corner of you,
there's a memory of spring,

of light,
of the earth waking up again.
It's distant, like a dream you can't quite recall,
but it's there—
waiting with you
in the quiet.

In the glass

A bottle held like a secret,
a quiet promise that this time,
you'll only take a sip.
Just enough to blur the edges,
to turn down the volume
of the thoughts that won't stop.

But it's never just a sip.
The glass empties
and you pour again,
chasing a numbness
that feels like safety
until it swallows you whole.

Your hands shake when it's gone,
your mind screams when it's near,
and the cycle spins faster,
pulling you under
while you smile through the haze,
convincing everyone
you're still in control.

But you know the truth—
it owns you now,
your body aching for another hit,
your soul shrinking beneath the weight
of every promise you broke
just to feel okay
for a little while longer.

Shifts

The room spins
before you can name it
an emergency.
Eyes dart for exits
that don't exist,
hands fumble for
anchors in air.

Crisis doesn't knock;
it bursts in,
uninvited,
demanding all your strength
in a single breath.
You lock eyes with yourself
in the mirror,
a face both yours
and not yours,
clinging to the seconds
like lifeboats.

And then,
a deep inhale,
a pause before
the sirens scream.
You root yourself
in the small things:
the quiet hum of a friend's voice,
the weight of your body
pressed to the earth,
the reminder
that even trembling hands
can hold on.

Even in the mess,
you are still here.

Nuckelavee

From the sea it rises,
night-bound and nameless,
a beast made of fear
and famine.
Horse's body,
man's torso fused above it,
skin stretched so thin
you see veins like rivers
pulsing black poison.
Its breath—salt rot and blight—
curling around the crops,
twisting life into death.
It is storm and hunger,
hoofbeats pounding out
a dirge of the inevitable.
This is no legend
for children's bedtime whispers;
it is the cry of the earth
when the balance tips,
the howling of winds
when humanity digs too deep.
But even terror
has its weakness.
The sea, its mother,
calls it back.
A single fresh stream
runs clean like defiance,
sending the beast fleeing,
reminding us
that even horrors
can drown
when truth flows strong.

In the face of the Nuckelavee,
we learn to plant hope
in salted ground
and pray it grows.

Tornado Season

There's a hum in the air—
the kind that finds its way into your bones,
makes your pulse stumble,
turns your hands into questions.
It's tornado season,
the sky wearing bruises,
thick and purple as something warning you
not to look too close.

Every year it feels like a test,
the way we watch the clouds gather
as if they're conspiring,
the way the world stills itself,
draws in its breath,
like it knows what's coming
and can't quite bear to watch.

This is how it goes,
a churn of thunder, a slap of wind,
and you're waiting for the sirens,
for the blast that says, *take cover,*
that says, *hold tight to what you love*
because you might not have the chance again.

In the basement, huddled close,
we're wrapped in the knowing
that everything we built
could be lifted and scattered,
that nothing we hold is promised,
that survival is just as fragile
as the faith we put into four walls.

But even in this thick quiet,

this trembling waiting,
something in us stands tall,
like a tree knowing its roots,
like a house that's been patched too many times
but still holds.

Tomorrow, maybe, the storm will pass,
and we'll step outside to the light—
to wreckage and wonder,
to pieces of ourselves thrown
but still here,
still looking for sky.

And isn't that what we are—
a map of losses, a list of rebuilds,
the proof of every time we stood
and said, "I'll hold,
I'll hold even if the wind decides
to call my name,
to test how much I can bend."

It's tornado season,
and still, we press our palms
to the earth, to the walls,
to each other, saying,
I'm here, I'm here,
in case that's enough

Part Two
Healing

Somewhere in-between

There's a map in my chest
with folds so worn they blur the ink—
paths I took to survive,
bridges I burned, forests I ran through,
each step a rhythm of fear and fight.

But some roads are too heavy to carry.
The weight of them pulls against my ribs,
my breath, a whispered plea: *Let it go.*
And still, my hands tremble—
not ready to release what once saved me.

Because self-care isn't soft.
It's a blade that cuts through excuses,
a fire that burns down comfort
to build safety from the ashes.

Holding on is a choice.
Letting go, a promise.
And somewhere between
the opening fist and the open road,
there's a life waiting for you
to honor it.

Blue Christmas

Blue is not the color they show you in the ads,
but it shows up anyway,
slipping in under the doorframe,
perching in the corner of the room,
pressing its weight into the stillness of December nights.
Blue is the absence and the ache,
the empty seat at the table,
the gift unwrapped because they are no longer here.
It is the chorus of "Silent Night"
sung by voices too full of loss to carry a melody.
They told us this season is for joy,
but joy has its own rhythm,
and sometimes it arrives late,
limping,
wearing a face you do not recognize.
We are told to shine brighter,
to stuff the silence with glitter,
to drown out the grief with carols and cheer,
but some nights, blue is all there is.
And that is holy too.
For blue holds the memory,
blue cradles the space where love still lingers,
blue teaches us to sit,
to breathe,
to feel.
So let the blue be the candlelight,
soft and steady.
Let it hold your hand
until the dawn begins to stretch across the horizon—
not in golds and reds,
but in the quiet promise of a softer shade.
This season is wide enough for every color,

even the ones that ache,
even the ones that wait for healing
just around the bend of the longest night.

Suicide Prevention

We stand here,
in a field of what feels like nothing—
soil cracked,
hearts brittle from the weight of silence.
But I've seen hands like yours,
trembling, unsure,
press seeds into this ground,
even when it seemed impossible.

And isn't that what hope is?
To plant when all you know is drought,
to water when the clouds refuse to gather,
to believe in roots
even when all you can see is dust?

I know the dark can be heavy,
pressing down like the weight of a thousand nights
that feel like they will never end.
But I promise,
there's light waiting
on the other side of this horizon.

Your story isn't over,
it's just in its winter.
And winter is not forever—
it's the resting,
the slow and unseen gathering of strength
for what will bloom.

So today, we plant.
Even if your hands shake.
Even if you feel like letting go.
We plant the seeds of tomorrow,

whisper to the earth,
"I am still here."

One day, you'll look back,
and where you thought there'd be nothing,
there will be wildflowers.
Proof that you stayed,
proof that hope is something we grow,
even when we can't yet see its bloom.

And when the night presses in,
know this:
you are not alone.
There are hands beside you,
planting, too.
Together, we are a garden,
and we will rise,
rooted in hope,
blooming in the light of another day.

Droplets

The air hums damp,
smelling of moss and earth's heartbeat,
the kind of wet that clings to your skin
and reminds you—
water is life.

Each droplet a prayer,
each root a hymn reaching down
to sip the melody.
The forest breathes in cycles,
and we, small creatures,
are lucky to inhale its song.

Social Media

The screen hums, a restless heartbeat,
but your own has been whispering, enough.
Step back—
the world doesn't dissolve
when you stop scrolling.
There's a quiet sky waiting
with stars not asking for likes,
and a sun rising just for you,
no algorithm required.
Let the silence
be the only post you make today.

I Choose

I choose the softness of your voice
when the world is too loud.
I choose the way your hand finds mine
like it's always known where to go.
I choose the mornings
that start with coffee,
and the nights that end
in the quiet space between us,
the kind of silence
that doesn't need to be filled
because it's already enough.
I choose the fight.
The ugly, messy, rawness of it.
I choose to stay when the easy thing
would be to walk away.
I choose the tears,
the anger,
the way we don't always understand
each other,
but we keep trying anyway.
I choose your laugh,
the one that breaks through my walls
like light pouring through the cracks
in everything I thought I had to be.
I choose the way you see me
in the moments I don't even see myself,
the way you remind me
I'm enough
even when I can't feel it.
I choose the mundane,
the everyday grocery lists,
the dishes in the sink,
the socks left on the floor

(because yes, you always do).
I choose the life we build
out of the small things,
the way they pile up
into something that feels like home.
I choose the future
that neither of us can see.
I choose the questions,
the uncertainty,
the steps we take
without knowing where they lead
but trusting the ground will hold us
if we hold on to each other.
I choose you,
and tomorrow, I'll choose you again,
in all your imperfections,
in all your beauty,
in all the ways we keep breaking open
and growing together.
Because marriage isn't a single choice.
It's a million little choices,
every day,
every moment.

Ear Worm Carols

Begin again in silence—
not the thunder of praise,
but the breath before the first word,
the ache before the first note.
This is where the story starts:
with darkness hovering over the deep,
with questions written in the margins of ancient scrolls,
with a song no one dared to sing.
"Once upon a time," they tell us,
"all was perfect,"
but we know better.
We know how the threads have frayed,
how the verses have cracked
under the weight of exclusion,
how the carols, sung too loud,
can drown out the weeping.
What if the lessons were lessons for us,
not just a recounting of long-ago miracles
but a mirror held to the systems we've built?
What if the candles flickering in the dark
are calling us to kindle justice,
not just in a Bethlehem stable
but in every sanctuary, every street?
Sing the Magnificat as if Mary is still crying out:
scatter the proud,
lift the lowly,
fill the hungry.
Let the melody rise like protest,
like hope breaking open the silence,
like a promise we can no longer ignore.
We have mistaken tradition for truth,
wrapped oppression in garlands,
hung injustice on the tree.

But this night,
this unraveling night,
asks us to lay it all bare—
the gold, the tinsel, the storylines
we tell ourselves to avoid the harder work.
And when the choir begins again,
may the song be new.
May it stitch together
what the systems have torn apart.
May it gather every voice,
even the ones we have silenced.
This is the carol for the weary world,
not just a hymn of longing,
but a blueprint for repair.
And the chorus?
It begins with us.

Confetti

The confetti settles
like tiny paper promises
on the cracked hardwood floor,
where last year's resolutions
still lie half-broken,
where laughter meets
the edge of regret,
and tears dry
in the glow of fairy lights
you meant to take down in March.

You toast to another try,
the clock's relentless tick
echoing inside you,
reminding you that time
is just another way to say
keep moving
even when you don't know
where the path ends.

Life spills over the sides,
red wine stains on your best dress,
shouts from the street below,
a song half-sung,
a hand held out.
This is how you carry hope:
with fingers smudged with ink,
with feet that trip and rise,
with a heart that aches
but still opens
at the sound of the next sunrise.

The Gospel of Trees

The trees don't stand alone,
though it looks that way at first glance—
a choir of soloists, each branch
lifting its hymn to the sky.
But below, beneath the dirt's dark lid,
their roots are writing a love story
that no one ever taught them to tell.

It begins with touch—
a tangle of fingertips feeling
for the pulse of the forest.
It's not competition, it's communion:
the way oaks send sugar
to birches bowed in shadow,
the way maples whisper warnings
when fire breathes too close.
One tree falling
does not mean silence.

The mycelium moves like memory,
a thousand miles of connection,
every thread a reminder
that strength is only strength
when it is shared.
You don't have to see it
to know it's there,
the way you don't see breath
but still feel its weight
when a loved one exhales it
into your arms.

The trees have always known this:
how to belong to each other.
How to live as a forest
instead of a single, trembling trunk.
Every storm survived
is because they held on—
not just to the ground,
but to each other,
their roots whispering,
I have you. I will not let you go.

When lightning comes,
it's not the tallest tree
but the ones closest to it
that break.
Sacrifice isn't something they choose—
it's instinct.
The gospel of trees is simple:
give what you have
until there is nothing left to give.
And even then,
your body will feed the earth,
your roots will braid into theirs,
your fall will not be the end of the story.

This is how the forest survives:
not by standing tall,
but by bending low enough
to hold the ones beside you.

Stability

In a room
where voices collide,
where the air trembles
with arguments
and the clatter of breaking news,
you reach for a moment,
a pause,
the half-second between beats
that whispers,
"You are here."

Your hands shake
but you place them
on the table,
steady and firm.
You gather the pieces
of noise,
of fear,
of everything that blurs
the edges of your name,
and you lay them down gently.

This is how you find it:
not by silencing the storm,
but by standing still,
until you become
the eye of it.

Tis the Season

Right now,
life is spilling over the edges,
like a too-full cup,
and I am both drowning in it
and learning how to swim.

Chaos,
like clothes piled on a floor I swear I'll clean tomorrow,
like phone calls I don't want to answer,
emails left unopened,
a calendar scribbled with too many things to be done,
and me, caught somewhere in the middle,
trying to remember how to breathe.

But this—
this is a season,
not a lifetime.
I whisper it to myself
like a prayer I don't yet believe,
but I'm holding onto it anyway,
because I've learned the difference
between forever and now.

There's healing here, too,
in the cracks between all the noise,
in the way I let myself pause
just long enough
to feel the sun on my face,
to let the rain wash away what I can't carry.

Discernment sits quietly in the corner,
not in the form of answers,
but questions,
gently nudging me,
asking,
"What matters right now?"
"What can be let go?"

And in the letting go,
there's renewal.
Not like a flood,
but a slow drip,
like water finding its way through stone,
like the earth thawing after a long winter.
I don't have to rush the bloom—
it will come.

This is the season of fullness,
of feeling too much,
of learning how to hold it all
without breaking.
But it's not the only season.
It's just the right now.
And I am learning to trust
that after the chaos,
comes the quiet.

After the storm,
comes the stillness
where we gather ourselves,
where we name what is ours to carry,
and what we can finally set down.

And when that stillness comes,
I will stand in it,
knowing that this was the season
that taught me how to bend,
how to heal,
how to grow.

Church Undone

We sit in pews woven from centuries,
threads of power and prayer interlocked.
But when I run my hand across the surface,
I feel the snags—racism, sexism,
colonialism, ableism,
threads spun so tight they strangle breath
but call it holy.
They tell us unity means silence,
that questioning is breaking,
but I say breaking is the first act of mending.
Because what good is a body
that cannot bleed truth?
I see the isms stitched into hymns,
woven through stained glass stories
where women speak only to birth or weep,
where whiteness paints halos
and blackness is cast as sin.
I see them cloaked in tradition,
bent beneath pulpits that demand allegiance
but refuse accountability.
So, I pull.
Not because I want to destroy,
but because the God I know
moves in the unraveling.
In the undoing of what was never divine,
in the loosening of power
until the fabric can breathe again.
Let the church come undone,
until every thread finds its rightful place—
no longer choking, but holding,
no longer silencing, but amplifying.
And when it's done,

when the isms are unspooled,
we will weave anew—
a tapestry wide enough for all to rest beneath,
stitched with hands that tremble,
but know they're building something sacred.

After the Storm

When the earth cracks, when the sky screams,
we stand—hearts trembling like leaves in a storm—
asking the same question:
How do we rise when the ground beneath us crumbles?
How do we hope when the floods come,
carrying away everything we thought was ours?
We were never taught to swim in sorrow,
never taught to dance in the dark,
but still—we learn.
With every shudder, every aftershock,
we gather our fear like kindling,
and we burn a fire bright enough
to see through the smoke of what's been lost.
Because even as the winds howl,
even as the waters rise,
we know that hope is a seed
buried deep in the soil of our souls,
and it will bloom—even after the storm.
The sky can tear open, the seas can roar,
but inside us, there is a quiet that refuses to be silenced.
It is the voice that says:
You are still here.
You have always been here.
We've learned to count the stars in a sky heavy with ash,
to hold each other's hands when the fires come,
and when we don't know if tomorrow will stand
or collapse like a wave upon the shore,
we still dare to whisper:
Tomorrow, we rise.
Because hope isn't the absence of fear—
it's the defiant drumbeat beneath it,
the pulse of a heart that says,
"We will rebuild,

even if the walls fall down."
So when the earth shakes,
when the waters rise,
when all we've known becomes the dust we walk upon—
    remember this:
we are more than survivors.
We are the architects of a new dawn.
The ground trembles, but we do not fall.
The storm rages, but we hold on to each other,
knowing that in the breaking,
we are reborn.

Unraveling Systems

There's a thread in the flag
that's been pulling loose for centuries,
red stained with stolen lands,
white woven with stolen labor,
blue so dark it's drowning.
We've been told it's treason to tug at it,
to question the fabric that drapes our lives—
but what's patriotism if not
unweaving the lie for the sake of truth?
The systems call themselves seamless,
but they are patched with the sweat
of mothers who fed children from empty plates,
stitched with the prayers of workers
bent double in fields
and never paid enough to dream.
Their edges fray
where humanity rubs too hard against profit,
where bodies break for another's gain.
And isn't that the lesson
we were always meant to learn?
That repair begins
where we let it all come undone?
That the only thing worth saving
is the part that says everyone deserves
to be held whole?
The unraveling isn't the end;
it's the beginning,
the place where our hands finally meet—
to pull, to mend, to create a world
where no one's pain
is the price of someone else's comfort.

Resilience

There will come a day
when the light between us flickers
like the dying bulb in the hallway
and I will be
both terrified and tender,
bracing myself for the moment
you forget my name.
I'll watch the cracks spread wide across our mornings—
coffee cups shaking in hands that once knew
exactly how to hold each other.
We'll be ghosts in the kitchen,
moving around the memories we've made,
and I'll remind you, again,
of the song we used to sing when we were kids,
but it won't reach you,
not like it used to.
How do I prepare
for the day your eyes
don't recognize the walls you built?
For the way the ground will open up
beneath us both,
and you'll tumble down the hole
where your memories used to live?
I've tried to map the route back to you,
but the landscape shifts
like the wind never learned
how to settle.
And I can't fix this.
I can't stitch together what's unraveling
inside your mind,
even though I'd break all my bones
just to hold you in place.

There's a cruelty in time,
how it teases us—
gives us decades
just to steal the last years,
when we're most tender,
when we need each other most.
We spend our lives
learning to love
just to lose what we've learned
in the end.
But even then—
even when you forget the name
you whispered in my ear
on the darkest nights,
when the world was too much
and all we had was this—
I will still say it.
I will write your name in the sand
just to watch it fade,
again and again,
because what else is love
but learning to lose?
I'll keep calling out,
even when you can't answer,
even when the only thing left
is the silence between us.
Because I won't let this disappear.
I won't let you vanish
without a fight.
And maybe, in that moment—
when the world goes dim,
and the last thread breaks—
we will still be here,
holding each other,
even in the forgetting.

Because love is the thing
that stays,
even when you don't.

For Yom Kippur

There is a sacred silence in the air,
a stillness that stretches across time,
and in this moment, we pause—
not as separate paths, but as branches
woven from the same root.
Today, the world listens,
as you gather in the shadow of ancient prayers,
your hearts turned toward the sky,
your souls like candles flickering
in the presence of something vast,
something holy.
We see you—our Jewish siblings—
wrapped in the light of this Day of Atonement,
and we are with you,
bearing witness to your journey.
The weight of the year rests on your shoulders,
each sin, each sorrow, each unspoken word
laid before the Divine.
And in this act, there is a beauty we can feel
deep in our bones:
the power of confession,
the grace of repentance,
the holiness of renewal.
For we, too, know the language of forgiveness,
have walked the path where brokenness becomes whole.
And so, as you fast,
as you pray,
as you seek the face of God in the quiet of your hearts,
we honor the courage it takes
to lay yourself bare
before the Divine.
We do not push apart from this sacred day—
but beside you,

our prayers weaving with yours,
our hearts leaning in,
we acknowledge we are kin,
tied by a covenant older than any of us,
by a promise that transcends borders,
by a faith that calls us to remember—
always—
that we are bound by more than belief.
So as you rise from the ashes of the past year,
as you seek forgiveness for what has been,
may you feel our hands beneath your feet,
our love in the breath between your words,
lifting you toward mercy.
And when the gates close at twilight,
when the shofar sounds across the evening sky,
know that we, too, are renewed.
For your prayers are a light to the world,
and in your atonement,
we are all reminded—
that grace is a gift given freely,
and in our shared humanity,
we rise together.
On this day of sacred reflection,
we honor you.
We stand beside you,
in awe of the beauty
of this moment.
Together, we seek what is holy,
together, we find peace.

Monday

It's all too much—
the stack of dishes tipping over,
the checkbook we never balanced,
the sky itself, relentless,
churning up another storm,
because it can, because it must,
because nature feels everything,
feels us.
And here we are,
arms barely holding
the pieces of ourselves we once promised
to protect—
small, trembling fragments
we polish and prop up each day,
telling ourselves it's enough.
But each morning looks like the one before,
and somehow we're on repeat,
coffee cup to dirty dish,
clock to unread book,
the space between us and yesterday
shrinking with each hour.
The days are blurring like a watercolor left in the rain—
colors bleeding, edges dissolving,
our plans ink-washed down to empty shades of intention.
We're breathing, yes,
but barely.
We're a list half-checked,
a pile of nearlys,
a thousand things we wanted to fix
but set aside
because
it was all too much.
So maybe today, we let go.

Drop one thing, or two,
watch them hit the ground—
whatever decides to stay whole
is what we'll call worthy,
is what we'll call ours.
We'll learn to live with what's left,
to love the bones of ourselves,
even if they're splintered,
even if they hold us
only because we asked them
one more time.
And in that small space,
the one we thought was loss,
something steady—
maybe peace,
maybe the kind of hope
that doesn't care
if it blurs into tomorrow

Women's March

We were born with fire in our throats,
and every time we open our mouths,
the world has a way of getting warmer.
Today, the streets hold us like an open wound,
our feet moving over concrete, softening the hard places,
turning pain into purpose, heartbreak into hymn.

Each step is a revolution,
the sound of a thousand bodies
daring the ground to forget us.
We march with hope, stretched so thin
it's almost invisible—yet somehow, it holds.

Because hope is a stubborn thing,
the kind that doesn't mind being tired,
the kind that gets knocked down and rises again,
one blistered foot in front of the other.

We march for the sisters we know
and the ones we don't. For our mothers,
whose hands have always been calloused
from holding up the weight of a world
that never seemed to fit right on their shoulders.
For the daughters yet to be born,
whose names we tattoo into this pavement,
an act of faith in a future they deserve.

And yes, we are tired.
Tired of asking, of shouting, of crying,
but here we are, standing anyway,
a sea of bodies becoming a wave.

Because change doesn't come easy,

but it comes—
it comes in steps, in chants, in open hands
and clenched fists, in voices that crack
but keep singing, that break but keep building.

We are marching for every 'no' that turned to 'yes',
for every door shut, now wide open.
This is not just a step; it's a promise,
the kind you make when the night feels endless,
but you believe morning is worth the wait

Living in Lament

We live in a world where grief is an anthem,
an echo that follows each morning light,
where the news blares with wounds
we've come to recognize by name,
where justice seems a mirage in the distance,
and our hearts learn the shape of heavy
before they learn anything else.
We sit in the quiet of sorrow,
hands clenched, bones weary,
lamenting the way cruelty stitches itself
into laws, into policies, into the cold machinery
that crushes the spirit and calls it order.
It's the kind of ache that wakes you at 2 a.m.,
when you remember the weight of all
that's been taken, all that's been lost.
And yet, there is something holy
in this grief, in this lament,
something fierce and alive,
that says, "This is not the end."
It is the drumbeat beneath the tears,
a knowing that mourning is not weakness
but a fuel, a rallying cry,
a deep, rumbling promise
to the oppressed, the silenced, the broken.
So let us sit with her—Lament—
like an old friend,
clinging tightly to her truth,
because she is the mother of every fight
we have yet to win,
the heartbeat behind the roar of protest,
the strength that steadies shaking hands
when we reach out,
to lift each other, to push back

against the weight of a world
that forgot how to hold its own heart.
We hold on to her,
because in her shadow, we remember
what we're fighting for:
the sacred worth of every soul,
a world that doesn't just breathe
but sings, free and whole.
We learn from her, rise with her,
so that when dawn breaks,
we are ready, fire in our eyes,
to take the fight back
to the places that harm, oppress,
and kill the light of humanity.
Hold her close,
because in her embrace,
we find our strength,
our voice,
our reason
to rise, again and again,
to fight for what must be changed.

Season of in-between

November exhales,
a final breath of brittle leaves and frost-bitten mornings.
The sun dips early,
casting its long shadows as a quiet farewell.
This is the season of in-between,
where the trees stand bare but patient,
their arms lifted to skies that promise
both snow and the return of light.
We hold the last day softly,
fingers tracing its edges,
knowing the year grows heavy in its final stretch.
Let us linger here,
in the quiet dusk of November,
where endings and beginnings blur,
and time feels like a whispered prayer.

Part Three
Renewal

Rebuke it ALL

In the shadows of tomorrow, and the chaos of yesterday,
   there's talk of despair,
Whispers of division, heavy hearts broken wide open.
A stage set for chaos, where truth's often bent,
But I say,
I rebuke it.
Theres talk of a future built on fear,
Of walls rising high while compassion becomes mere
   crumbs under the table that only the dogs will eat.
But love is our armor, and unity's our vow,
So I say,
I rebuke it.
The echoes of hatred, they try to cling to our bones, our
   spirits
Claiming that silence is safety,
But our voices are thunder, our spirits the indicators of
   our humanity,
So with courage as our anthem, I say,
I rebuke it.
And while there's time for courage,
and still fight left to be had
For the world we dream of
My resolve is steady for this moment
To proclaim,
I rebuke it this day.

It all Returns

I have watched the earth turn itself inside out,
seen the sky fold like laundry over tired hands,
each season a stitch in the fabric of becoming
that unravels just when you think
you've got it sewn up tight.

We are born, we break, we bloom again.
Not in straight lines,
but in circles—
the kind you can trace with your fingertip
on the surface of a pond,
a ripple bending outward,
coming back home.

I used to think healing meant an end,
like crossing a finish line with scars
that stayed closed,
like you could stitch your heart shut
and say, *that's done now.*
But the truth is, we are constantly remaking ourselves,
over and over,
a garden that dies
only to push itself up through the soil,
year after year,
blossoms cracking through frost.

It's not the breaking that ends us,
it's the forgetting that we are more than our wounds,
more than the fall of leaves,
more than the branches snapped under the weight
of everything we carry.

Watch how the trees shed what no longer serves them,

how they let go because they know
there is more to come,
that growth is a cycle, not a destination,
and maybe we should follow their lead—
stand still in the mess of it all,
and trust that spring will return
even if the winter feels endless.

We think we're broken,
but we're just seeds waiting for the right moment
to split open,
for the water to reach us.

You are not a finished thing,
not yet,
and that's the most beautiful part.
Everything you are is still growing back,
the garden, the root, the bloom—
it all returns,
if you let it.

Winter Hymn

The wind bites like it has teeth,
gnaws at the edges of breath,
presses its chill against the ribs
like it's searching for cracks.
This is winter's hymn—
not soft, but sharp.
A bitter aria,
whistling through bare branches
and shaking the bones of the earth.
You pull your coat tighter,
face turned from its fury,
but the song keeps chasing,
a reminder
that not all beauty
is warm.

Burnt

The air tastes like ash,
a language no one asked to learn.
Smoke curls around the mountains,
a grief too big to hold in your lungs.
Every tree becomes a ghost of itself,
every horizon smudged
with the fingerprints of a fire
that knows no mercy.
The earth,
once a cradle of green,
now whispers in charred tones:
remember me.
Neighbors become lifelines,
eyes watering not just from smoke,
but from the sight of homes
splintering into memory.
And still,
the crows keep circling.
The sun sets like it always does,
bloody and bold,
a reminder that even endings burn.

We're a Part of it

The air hums damp,
smelling of moss and earth's heartbeat,
the kind of wet that clings to your skin
and reminds you—
water is life.

Each droplet a prayer,
each root a hymn reaching down
to sip the melody.
The forest breathes in cycles,
and we, small creatures,
are lucky to inhale its song

Above the Clouds

Up here, the earth becomes
a quilt someone forgot to finish—
fields stitched in uneven squares,
rivers threading silver through the seams,
cities dotting the fabric like stray buttons.
From this height,
the highways stop roaring,
the houses stop shouting,
the inbox stops buzzing in my skull.

I can see everything
but touch nothing.
And it feels like relief—
like someone hit pause
on the chaos below.

From this distance,
there are no overdue notices,
no cracked phone screens,
no dishes balancing like bad decisions
in the sink.
There is only the horizon
stacked in colors too soft for worry:
gold bleeding into rose,
a blue so tender it forgets
to be sky.

The plane bumps,
and my stomach tumbles,
a reminder that I am still small,
still human, still carried
by something much larger than myself.
Gravity holds its hands out beneath me,

just in case.

Perspective is not found,
it is borrowed—
a gift from the altitude.
Down there, I am an ant
shouldering the world.
Up here, I am only a speck
drifting through air
and possibility.

The fields blur into a mosaic.
The rivers become veins,
pulsing life into land.
I think of how tiny my problems must look
from this high up,
how maybe, just maybe,
they too are part of the pattern.

The plane begins its descent,
clouds closing over the view
like a curtain.
Soon, I'll be back in the noise,
the scramble,
the ordinary everything.
But for now, I carry this quiet:
a pocket-sized horizon,
a quilt stitched with distance,
a promise that not every moment
has to feel so impossibly heavy.

Invitation to Thresholds

There's a tremble in the ask,
a catch in the throat of the word *welcome,*
because how do you invite someone to the place
that once burned them—
call it hearth, call it home—
when the ashes still cling to your hands?

We're building something new here,
but the ghosts don't care about blueprints.
They hover in the rafters,
in the shadows of songs sung off-key by systems
that turned healing into hymns for themselves.

So we honor the wound.
We do not cover it with gilded invitations.
We say:
"I see the scar and how it pulses under the light.
I see the hurt still etched in your name."

This is not a clean slate,
but maybe it's a softer ground
where we can plant something
that doesn't force roots through cracked bones.

If you come,
bring the ache with you,
bring the questions,
bring the sharp edge of your *no.*
This space is not afraid to hold it.

And if you stay away,
that too is holy,
because healing cannot be summoned like a ghost

and trust is not a thing rebuilt with words
but with time.

Still, the door is open.
The wound does not close it.
We sit at the threshold,
tending the fire,
waiting—
not for the wound to vanish,
but for the weight of it to be shared.

Tiny Miracles

It is always moss—
always the soft green cradle
spreading like a whisper
beneath the noise of trees.
While the canopy shouts at the sun,
the moss hums a secret hymn,
its language small enough to miss
unless you kneel to listen.

Here, the world shifts.
The sky becomes a memory,
your worries, too big to carry,
shrink down to spores.
Every leaf-tip,
every tiny branch
a reminder that greatness
is not size
but presence—
the way moss claims its space
without needing to prove
it's worth the water.

This is a universe
you could hold in your palm—
a hundred lives
dancing on a thread of dew,
each one saying,
Look closer. Here is where beauty lives.
Here is where miracles grow quietly.

You don't have to be the tallest
to reach the light.

Sometimes,
being closest to the ground
is how you learn
to carry the weight
of the whole forest.

Before an election

Today, I choose to breathe,
even with the weight of a nation pressing down on my
    chest,
even when the headlines scream like sirens,
and truth feels like a casualty
in a war no one admits we're fighting.
I sit with the fear,
the kind that creeps in between conversations,
disguised as silence but thick with division.
It lingers in the spaces between us,
where politics crack open the ground
we thought was common,
but now feels foreign, broken,
like a language we no longer speak.
I hear the propaganda,
the lies dressed up in promises
meant to keep us small, scared,
pitted against each other
as if we are enemies,
as if the lines drawn on maps
or screens can define the whole of who we are.
But today, I choose to breathe.
To inhale hope,
exhale fear,
and believe that beneath the noise,
there is still something worth saving.
A country, a heart,
a conversation waiting to happen.
I don't close my eyes.
I watch the storms brewing,
the anger, the distrust,
the fear that says, "You don't belong here."
But I open myself to the wind,

to the possibility that what's yet to come
might be bigger than the chaos
we're drowning in now.
Today, I choose to remember
that we survive by staying open—
by listening when it's hard,
by seeing each other
when we've been taught to look away.
Because today isn't the end.
Today is just one step,
and what's coming could still be light
if we choose to keep the doors unlocked
and our hearts soft enough
to hold a future we can't yet see.
So today, I breathe.
And I believe.

Remembering Sabbath

In the hush between heartbeats,
where the world softens its edges,
there lies a sacred pause,
an invitation to breathe,
to let the soul unfurl its wings
and settle into the embrace of stillness.
Here, time doesn't tick—it dances,
spinning in slow motion,
as we shed the weights of "should" and "must,"
replacing them with the gentle knowing
that to rest is to honor the pulse of life,
to weave joy into the fabric of the ordinary.
Sabbath, a whispered promise,
calls us to the table of presence,
to feast on the simple, the profound—
the laughter of friends, the light in a child's eyes,
the sound of rain against window panes,
where quiet becomes a canvas
for the colors of our longing and delight.
Let us light candles of gratitude,
let our hearts be the offering,
offering our ache for rest
and our thirst for connection,
as we melt into this gentle grace,
cradled by the rhythm of what's essential,
the art of simply being,
of soaking in the sacredness of the now.
So, let the world wait, let it whirl and spin,
for here in this sanctuary of silence,
we gather the pieces of who we are,
learning that rest is not an escape,
but the fertile ground where hope blooms,
where love whispers its softest truths.

In the stillness of now, we remember—
we are not just human doings, but human beings,
and the sweetest liberation lies
in the pause, the breath,
the sacred space of rest,
our bodies and spirits
finding home again.

Yuletide Exhale

It's Yuletide,
and the world feels like it's exhaling—
a slow, spiraling breath into the lungs of the longest night.
The fire doesn't just crackle; it sings,
a hymn to everything that endures:
the pine bending under snow,
the holly daring the frost,
the oak giving itself to the hearth.
We hang wreaths like ancient prayers,
circles unbroken, whispers of sun's return.
We drink spiced cider like it's memory,
like it knows the stories we've forgotten to tell.
Here, the dark is a cradle, not a coffin.
We rock ourselves in its stillness,
knowing the stars are rebuilding.
Every ember sparks a promise:
the light will come back,
but first, let us honor the shadow.

Hopeless hope…(inspired by LOTR)

There's a moment when you realize
what you thought you needed to survive
was never the heavy things.
The cast-iron pans,
the tools that clanged like armor—
you leave them behind,
because there's no room for burden
when you're carrying the last shred of hope
the world has to offer.
And that's what it feels like, isn't it?
This hope, this thing you cradle in your palm,
light as dirt and just as fragile,
a gift from the kind of hands
that see the future
buried in the smallest things.
You think about what it means
to trade survival for something that grows,
to leave behind the comfort of knowing
how to feed yourself today
and instead, carry the soil
that might save tomorrow.
You're not sure the world can be saved,
but you carry the dirt anyway.
That's how hopeless hope works—
you tend to what might never bloom.
So you trudge across barren lands,
with the scent of cooking fires
still lingering in your chest,
but the weight on your back feels lighter
because now you carry what can't be seen.
You carry the memory of a garden
that hasn't yet existed,

the green that will rise
from a place scorched and broken.
And when you reach the place
where the shadows finally stop,
you won't plant your feet,
you'll plant the seeds.
Because somewhere deep inside,
you know that the battle isn't just fought
with swords and courage,
but with roots that break through
even the hardest of ground.
You will press your hands into the soil
like a prayer,
and remember the taste of strawberries
before you knew what war was.
Before you knew what it meant
to live in a world where everything dies,
and still believe
that things can grow again.
This is your gift.
Not the strength of your arm,
or the fire in your belly,
but the quiet faith
that something small
can heal something vast.
That dirt, carried far enough,
can become home again.
So you plant.
You dig and bury,
and even if the sky doesn't break into bloom,
even if your hands never harvest what you sow,
there will be others—
those who come after,
those who never knew the hunger you felt,
who will walk barefoot on the soft ground

and thank you
for the garden
you never got to see.

Black Friday

On this day of hunger for more,
we see price tags as gospel,
worship the glow of screens,
and trample over ourselves
to claim what's fleeting.

Remember how the soil beneath the malls
once cradled seeds, not receipts.
How rivers, not parking lots,
reflected the sky's endless offering.

We are more than consumers.
We are caretakers, storytellers,
keepers of enough.

Let us pause before the frenzy,
breathe in the wealth of stillness.
For abundance isn't found
in the clamor of carts,
but in the quiet hands
we hold each other with.

Between the Years

In the hush between the years,
where laughter lingers like a ghost,
we gather our shadows,
wrap them in the warmth of flickering lights,
each tear a star,
each sigh a whispered prayer.
The world slows,
time drips like candle wax,
and we sit,
cradling the weight of what was,
dreaming of what might be,
finding solace in the soft ache of longing.
Here, in the quiet,
we learn to hold our hearts gently,
to embrace the stillness,
to let the past and future dance,
as we breathe in the fragile beauty
of this tender, fleeting moment.

Calling

The day you are called,
it won't feel like thunder
or trumpets,
but more like a whisper
you've been hearing your whole life.
The kind that's threaded through
every doubt,
every "why me?"
every moment you thought
you were too small to be chosen.

But there you are,
standing with trembling hands,
holding the weight of something
larger than yourself.
Larger than the church pews,
the hymns,
the stained glass windows
that have watched you grow.

This is not the holy light
you imagined,
no angel wings brushing your shoulders,
no celestial chorus—
just a room full of people,
and the quiet that feels like a door
cracking open.
You step through anyway.

Because you know,
deep in your bones,
this is not about perfection.
This is about showing up

with all your scars,
all your questions,
and still saying, "Yes."

Yes, even though your voice shakes,
even though you're afraid
of the weight this title carries,
even though the world tells you
that your voice is too small,
too queer,
too much,
or not enough.

But you know better.
You've been called by something
older than fear,
something louder than doubt.
And you are walking in it now,
arms open wide,
saying,
"I am here.
I am ready.
Send me."

And on that day,
the weight will lift.
Not because the road will be easy,
but because you know,
this is what you were made for—
to heal, to fight, to love
with every breath
of your being.

The day you are called,
it won't feel like you've arrived.
It will feel like you've just begun.

In Full Color

I used to think life was waiting,
some future version of myself
I had to reach,
some place ahead where things made sense,
where I had the answers,
where the chaos finally stilled.
But now, I see the gift was always
right here,
right now,
wrapped in the moment unfolding like breath.

The sky doesn't wait to be bluer tomorrow,
the wind doesn't ask for permission to blow.
The present is the only thing
we can truly hold—
and yet, we forget.
We rush past it,
eyes on the next step,
hands full of what's missing,
hearts holding the weight of what-ifs.

But today, I choose to be here—
to feel the ground beneath my feet,
the sun on my skin,
the sound of laughter
spilling like water in the air.

Today, I live with my hands wide open,
holding nothing but this second
before it slips into the next.

It's messy,
it's fleeting,
but it's real,
and it's mine.

So I take it—
in full color,
with all its imperfections,
and I breathe in this present moment,
the only one
that truly belongs to me.

The New Year

The year spins out
like thread from a spindle,
frayed at the edges,
knotted in the middle.
You sit at the table
where silence is company,
pen poised over paper,
wondering if this time
you'll write something
worth keeping.

You trace back the days,
each a chapter
scribbled with mistakes,
laugh lines,
unfinished dreams.
The mess of it all
sprawled out before you,
more beautiful
than you want to admit.

And as the midnight echoes,
fireworks catching the sky on fire,
you let out a breath
you didn't know you were holding.
A new start,
not clean,
but real.
Not perfect,
but yours.
And somewhere in the chaos,
you remember:

even tangled thread
can make something whole.

Prepared

Prepare ye the way of the Lord,
like you're clearing out the cobwebs
from a heart that's been too quiet,
like you're unrolling the sky for a revolution of stars.
Prepare ye,
because love never shows up unannounced.
It shouts through the wilderness,
whispers in the shadows,
sets a table for the outcast and calls it holy.
Prepare ye,
like justice is a guest you've waited your whole life to
    meet.
Sweep the floors, light the candles—
this is the moment everything changes.
Prepare ye the way of the Lord,
and watch as every valley rises to sing.

Samhain's Lullaby

Beautiful Samhain has arrived—
the Cailleach strikes her blackthorn staff
against earth thick with rot and root,
the hum of endings settles into soil,
sinks into our bones.

The light year closes.
Gone are the bright days of ripening fruit,
the loud green whispers of spring,
and now, only the soft, wet darkness
calls us inward.

It is the time of descent,
the time when wild things turn to silence,
and we too are urged to spiral down,
into the soil of ourselves,
toward the language without words,
the song of marrow and root.

A threshold waits at the edge of night,
its old wooden frame creaking open—
an invitation ancient as earth's bones,
asking us to pause,
to step away from the hurry and harvest,
to sit beside the shadow
we often turn from.

Because to enter the quiet is to strip bare,
to lay down every false name,
each heavy cloak of should and must,
and let them sink into compost,
let them decay into the dark.

For in the black soil of unknowing,
there is a voice, an ancient rhythm,
telling us we are cyclical, as wild as forest,
shifting, season-bound, we must descend
to find ourselves.

This is a death of sorts—
a sacred undoing, an offering of old ways
to the dark.

We look back at the soil we sprang from,
the stories held by roots,
the compost of ancestors,
and we remember—

This is not only a time for endings
but for honoring the long, quiet breath
of every beginning.

So tonight, we sing the songs of root and bone,
we sing the seeds that dream of spring.
We lay ourselves open to darkness
and let it fill us with the mystery of becoming,
of death as birth, of light as shadow,
of all that waits beneath.

Christmas Remade

We string up lights like safety nets,
hide behind glowing Santas and porcelain nativities,
as if nostalgia could drown out the cracks
in the walls we've built around this season.
There's a pageantry to it, isn't there?
Songs soaked in sugar,
traditions lacquered in a shine so thick
we can't see what's rotting beneath.
The push for perfect joy,
for smiles that stay pinned through the ache—
but joy isn't a mask,
and celebration shouldn't require sacrifice
of soul or sanity.
What of the ones left outside the snow globe?
The queer kid shut out of family gatherings.
The mother breaking under the weight
of buying what she can't afford.
The workers who get no rest
because profit doesn't celebrate Christmas.
They tell us it's tradition,
as if that word is an altar we dare not dismantle.
But tradition has hands,
and sometimes, they harm—
grasping, clinging to the past
instead of welcoming the future.
So, we unravel.
Untangle the garlands of guilt.
Unspool the hymns that silence.
Let the tinsel fall away
until all that's left is the raw, unvarnished truth:
this season is not owned by power
or marketed by greed.
It's a story of birth in a barn,

of light piercing the darkest night.
A reminder that the sacred
doesn't wear a price tag
or demand perfection.
Let us remake it—
a Christmas where the table is long,
the walls are gone,
and the joy is fierce enough
to set the world free.

Part Four
Becoming

Some Starts

Do not run toward the new
just because it shines.
Some seasons ask us to sit,
to feel the earth steady beneath us.
The future will wait,
its hands already reaching—
but today holds its own truths,
its own quiet revolution.

Shattered and Whole

It begins in chaos,
a storm of broken pieces
scattered at your feet.
Everything you thought you knew
about yourself, about love,
about how to carry pain—
it crumbles,
and you're left holding the fragments,
unsure what to save
and what to let slip
through your trembling fingers.

You think healing should be smooth,
a gentle unfolding,
but it's jagged.
It's messy.
It's nights spent questioning
if you're strong enough to keep going,
if the dark will ever lift,
if there's anything left inside you
worth saving.

Discernment comes slowly,
like the soft drip of rain
after a flood.
It's not clarity, not yet,
but it's a whisper in the silence,
a gentle nudge that says,
"You're still here.
Start again."

So you begin,
sifting through the wreckage,
holding each shard to the light
and asking,
"Is this mine?
Is this what I need
to rebuild?"

Some days,
the answer is no.

And you let it fall away,
watch it disappear into the past
with all the things
that no longer serve you.

Other days,
you find pieces of yourself
you'd forgotten.
Strength.
Grace.
The ability to breathe
even when the world feels like it's collapsing.
You gather them close,
tenderly,
like flowers you're planting
in a garden you never thought
would bloom again.

Renewal is not an arrival,
but a process—
a slow, steady waking.
A moment when you realize
you've made it this far,
and maybe, just maybe,
you're becoming someone new.

Someone softer,
but stronger.
Someone who knows that pain
isn't the end of the story,
but the soil where healing takes root,
where hope stretches its limbs
and begins to grow.

And you,
you are the gardener,
the caretaker of your own becoming,
learning to love
every phase of the bloom.

Krampus

Tonight, the shadows come to dance.
Krampus, hoof-heavy and grinning,
drags his chain-laden mischief through the streets.
This is no night for polished stars—
it's a reckoning, a reminder
that even in the season of light,
we carry our dark companions.
But oh, how alive it feels!
The crackle of fire,
the snarl of laughter,
the joy in knowing we're seen,
flaws and all, by something ancient
and wild.
It's a celebration of balance:
naughty meets nice,
fear shakes hands with awe.
We toast with mugs of mulled wine,
hearts lighter for the weight we've named.
So here's to Krampus,
keeper of the other side of cheer,
whose presence whispers:
you are whole,
and even your shadows
deserve a seat at the feast.

Stillness

A lake unmoving
is a mirror the world forgot to shatter—
the trees lean in to admire themselves,
the sky smears its blue into perfection.
It feels holy, almost,
a silence that hushes even the wind,
a surface too calm to trust.

But don't be fooled.
Still waters are liars.
Beneath that glassy façade,
depths yawn wide enough
to swallow light whole.
There is no map for what lies below,
no anchor that can touch
the bottom without trembling.

The quiet whispers secrets
you're not sure you want to hear.
Do fish glide through darkness like ghosts?
Do old tragedies sleep beneath the silt,
their edges softened by time?

What lives down there,
in the black beyond imagining?

From the shore,
you only see the beauty—
reflections too perfect to be real,
ripples that never come.
But step in,
and the cold will bite your skin,
pulling you deeper,

always deeper.

This is the paradox:
stillness can soothe
or suffocate.
It can hold you like a cradle
or like a trap.

The lake waits.
It offers nothing but itself—
an open palm,
an invitation to wonder,
to fear,
to dive,
or to simply walk away.

On Coming Out

In the tapestry of who we are,
Threads of laughter, love, and scars,
We acknowledge all of it.
Some stepping from the shadows
Some unable to,
Some dying to,
Some...dying...
All of us trying
To find spaces we belong.
For every whispered secret told,
For every heart that's brave and bold,
Let love be our anthem,
fierce and free,
A symphony of identities.
The beauty in the stories we weave
With open arms and hearts so wide,
We celebrate love,
and with it,
our pride.

Dilemma

There's a dance in the highs and lows,
the way life spins us—
arms flung wide on a carousel
that keeps speeding up, slowing down,
the thrill and the fear meeting in the middle,
that stuck place,
where you can't tell if you're holding on
or letting go.
It's where dilemmas live, I think—
those questions with too many answers
and none of them right,
or maybe all of them right,
and they cancel each other out,
leaving you here, breathless in the pause,
aching in the middle.
One moment, you're sky-high,
drunk on possibility,
drunk on hope, like somehow everything
might just make sense.
And the next?
You're down in the dirt,
scraping at rocks, digging a path to breathe,
to push through the mud
of all the "what ifs" that keep you grounded
right here.
And we're all here,
stuck in this space between—
where days feel like tightrope walks,
like balancing acts with no nets,
where one wrong word sends you spinning,
and one good laugh feels like it could save you.
This middle place, it's heavy,
it's too much of not enough,

it's a holding pattern of every decision
that brought you here.
But maybe, just maybe,
this middle place is its own answer,
the way silence fills the empty,
the way stillness holds the broken parts of us
together, just long enough
to remind us
that the middle is where life happens, too.

What's in a Name

It's not just a name—
it's a question shaped like a mirror that the world can see,
a word made of hopes and dreams and a whole lot more.
At the holiday table,
the name on your place card weighs differently
than the one the state stamps into their records,
the one they paste over your heartbeat,
like a too-small patch on a too-deep wound.
But under soft light and tinsel,
on a gift tag with handwriting you'd recognize
    anywhere—
your name, the real one, sits like a sigh,
like a homecoming.
It remembers who you are
when bureaucracies forget,
when letters from banks and utility companies and
    colleges
address a stranger
you've spent your whole life trying not to be.
Every name holds a story,
but not all names hold us back.
There's power in a gift tag—
someone wrote it who knows,
who sees you beyond the syllables.
So you slip it into your pocket,
hold it like a talisman,
a reminder that the world is a battlefield, yes,
but here, in these small spaces of recognition,
you can still plant flags of truth.
And maybe—just maybe—
the mailings, the IDs,
even the systems too rigid to understand

will one day learn to call you
by the name you've always been.

Permission to Pause

The bed becomes an ocean,
still and vast,
each breath a wave that says,
stay.
The world will wait.
Let the quiet cradle you,
let healing come not as a demand,
but as a tender whisper:
you are allowed to stop.

The Holidays

There's a battle that begins in the mirror,
a war between the version of you
that knows peace is priceless
and the one who's learned that peace,
at any cost, can carve out pieces
you don't get back.

The invitation sits on the table,
all glitter and hope,
etched with the names
of those who raised you
and those who don't know
the language of who you've become.

It's the holiday season,
the season when light tangles with darkness,
when homes hum with old songs,
and stories are revived
like ghosts pulled from
long-empty chairs.
And you stand at the door,
heart an open suitcase,
wondering what to pack.

To build a bridge
is to remember the shape of their hands,
the comfort of familiarity—
the way voices once lifted you
like sparrows
on the wings of childhood laughter.
But bridges are not built
without shaking foundations,
not without splinters

that linger long after the feast.

To stay away
is to preserve the heartbeat
of your own quiet,
to cradle your peace
with hands that no longer tremble
at raised voices
or sidelong questions
that cut like paper,
deep and without warning.

You think about love,
the double-edged word
that pulls you both ways:
toward the table,
toward the door.
You think about self-love,
how it tastes like freedom
and silence
and knowing
that boundaries can be both armor
and art.

And when the night falls,
when the moon wears its full face
and the stars look like eyes
you wish would just see you,
you let yourself pause.

Breathe into the ache
that holds both choices:
the longing to be known,
the need to stay whole.

Tonight, maybe you'll sit alone

and wrap yourself in music
that never asks you to choose.
Or maybe you'll cross that bridge,
your hands shaking,
your voice steadying
with each step.

Either way,
remember this:
even in the wrestling,
even in the indecision,
your love is still love,
and your heart,
no matter the distance,
is a home
that knows how to hold itself.

Darkness

The darkness comes early,
spreading like ink across the snow,
a quiet that stretches its arms wide,
inviting all the weary things
to fold themselves into the night.
These are the hours when stars hum softly,
when breath clouds the air,
and even the trees hold secrets
beneath their bare branches.
Winter asks us to stay,
to sit in its silence,
to let the weight of long nights
settle into our bones,
reminding us that rest is not empty,
but a seed,
rooting in the unseen.
What the dark holds,
it does not hoard.
It cradles the promise of light,
of return,
of a dawn that will come
only when we've learned
to trust the stillness.

Never alone

The trees don't stand alone,
though it looks that way at first glance—
a choir of soloists, each branch
lifting its hymn to the sky.
But below, beneath the dirt's dark lid,
their roots are writing a love story
that no one ever taught them to tell.

It begins with touch—
a tangle of fingertips feeling
for the pulse of the forest.
It's not competition, it's communion:
the way oaks send sugar
to birches bowed in shadow,
the way maples whisper warnings
when fire breathes too close.
One tree falling
does not mean silence.

The mycelium moves like memory,
a thousand miles of connection,
every thread a reminder
that strength is only strength
when it is shared.
You don't have to see it
to know it's there,
the way you don't see breath
but still feel its weight
when a loved one exhales it
into your arms.

The trees have always known this:
how to belong to each other.
How to live as a forest
instead of a single, trembling trunk.
Every storm survived
is because they held on—
not just to the ground,
but to each other,
their roots whispering,
I have you. I will not let you go.

When lightning comes,
it's not the tallest tree
but the ones closest to it
that break.
Sacrifice isn't something they choose—
it's instinct.
The gospel of trees is simple:
give what you have
until there is nothing left to give.
And even then,
your body will feed the earth,
your roots will braid into theirs,
your fall will not be the end of the story.

This is how the forest survives:
not by standing tall,
but by bending low enough
to hold the ones beside you.

The Whole of Us

Some days, the body whispers first—
a tightness in the chest,
a heaviness in the legs that feels like grief
but doesn't have a name yet.
Other days, it's the mind shouting,
a hurricane of thoughts spinning so fast
you can't tell where they started,
only that they want to pull you under.
And then there's the spirit,
waiting like a lighthouse—
steady, even in the fog,
its light brushing the edge of every wave.
Holistic health is the moment
you stop silencing one to hear the other.
It's the breath you take when the ache in your shoulder
reminds you how much you've been carrying,
how much you've been holding for too long.
It's the stillness that cradles you
until your mind loosens its grip
and your body trusts the ground beneath it again.
This is integration:
to sit in the center of your own being
and listen to every voice,
to bow to the wisdom in your scars,
to thank your heartbeat for never giving up,
to hear the spirit say,
"You are already whole—
even when you forget,
even when you break."
Healing isn't the goal.
It's the practice of remembering
that you are the world's most intricate ecosystem,

and every breath you take
keeps the forest alive.

Family Dynamics

There's a bruise where the dinner table used to be,
all knuckles and held breath,
voices breaking like dropped glass
at the mention of politics or prayer.

Home was once the hum of old stories,
stitched with laughter, the click
of silverware in familiar hands.
Now, it's the weight
of every unspoken name,
the silence between forkfuls
filling the room like smoke.

This is what it means to renegotiate family
when your humanity is up for debate—
when your love, your rights, your breath
become footnotes argued at the end
of an already fractured day.

You keep your heart close,
wrapped tight in the armor of learned patience,
pacing the perimeter of belonging,
wondering when you traded comfort
for cautious compromise.

They say blood is thicker than water,
but they forget
how blood has boiled
and how water can cleanse
and carry whole bodies downstream.

So, you find yourself
tending a garden inside your chest,
one that grows even when scorched by disbelief,
sowing seeds of the word 'enough'
with trembling fingers.

And still, there is faith—
in the patchwork love that endures
the storm of voices,
in the way your fingerprints
map out your place on this earth,
a silent testimony
to the moments you held the line
and dared to say,
"I'm still here."

Maybe today isn't the day
you convince them
that survival is not surrender.
But you learn to take a step back,
build a life where the echoes
of arguments don't
outweigh the music of your pulse.

And if your voice cracks
under the weight of explaining
again and again—
know this:
the tremor is not weakness;
it's the quaking ground
before roots break free
and a new story begins.

Liminal Space

The clock ticks louder when you're waiting,
like each second is a breath
held too long.
You pace the room
in small circles,
tracing hope in the lines of your palm,
wondering what words are coming
on the other end of the phone or chart or email.

Your heart beats in time with the silence,
thudding against your ribs,
carrying the weight
of every "what if" you've dared not speak.
But still, you wait,
because waiting is all you can do—
stand on the edge of knowing
and pray that when the news arrives,
it comes like rain,
gentle,
and not the storm you've feared.

Honor the Wound

There's a tremble in the ask,
a catch in the throat of the word welcome,
because how do you invite someone to the place
that once burned them—
call it hearth, call it home—
when the ashes still cling to your hands?
We're building something new here,
but the ghosts don't care about blueprints.
They hover in the rafters,
in the shadows of songs sung off-key by systems
that turned healing into hymns for themselves.
So we honor the wound.
We do not cover it with gilded invitations.
We say:
"I see the scar and how it pulses under the light.
I see the hurt still etched in your name."
This is not a clean slate,
but maybe it's a softer ground
where we can plant something
that doesn't force roots through cracked bones.
If you come,
bring the ache with you,
bring the questions,
bring the sharp edge of your no.
This space is not afraid to hold it.
And if you stay away,
that too is holy,
because healing cannot be summoned like a ghost
and trust is not a thing rebuilt with words
but with time.
Still, the door is open.
The wound does not close it.

We sit at the threshold,
tending the fire,
waiting—
not for the wound to vanish,
but for the weight of it to be shared.

Recouping

I cough so hard
that the world feels too small
to hold the weight of my aching lungs.
A fever blooms like a sunrise I didn't ask for,
my breath a whispered argument
with the air.
But the body—
oh, the body knows survival
better than I know surrender.
It fights in silence,
a million unseen battles,
reminding me that even in weakness,
there is a brilliance
to being alive

Endings

The day it ends,
it won't be the way you expected—
not like the closing of a book,
not like the final note of a song.
It will be quieter,
almost unnoticed,
like the breath you take
without realizing
it's the last of something.

Endings always slip through
in small moments.
They arrive without banners,
without the grand finale.
A phone call not returned,
the empty chair at the table,
the way your name
no longer lives on their lips.

And you thought you'd be ready.
Thought you'd see it coming,
but endings,
they are not loud.
They are the softness
of letting go,
the space between one thing
and the next
that feels too wide
to ever cross.

You'll stand there,
with hands that don't know what to hold,
and a heart too full of what's been lost.

But this is what endings do—
they leave room
for everything that's gone
and everything that's still
trying to make its way in.

And yes, you'll cry.
You'll rage at the unfairness,
at the silence left behind,
at how quickly life moves
from what was
to what will never be again.
But after that,
in the hollow of it all,
there will be something else—
something like peace,
something like a beginning
you didn't think was possible.

The day it ends,
you'll learn that endings
are not about what's taken,
but what's left behind.
A small seed of something
you didn't notice before,
waiting for you
to plant it.

And you'll hold it in your hands,
that fragile hope,
knowing that this, too,
will be the start of something
you never expected.

The Star

We are told to follow the star,
but no one warns us how small it might be—
a single word scrawled on a scrap of paper,
handed to you like a secret,
like a dare to see the divine
in the ordinary.
Hope, it says.
Or justice.
Or courage,
as if the syllables alone
can chart the course to Bethlehem,
to some inner sanctuary
where the world feels less jagged.
You hold it in your palm,
a compass disguised as ink and intention.
You wonder if the wise men doubted too,
if they looked up at the sky
and thought:
That can't be for me,
that light too distant,
the journey too long.
But stars don't wait for certainty,
they move with or without us.
They beckon,
not with guarantees,
but with the promise
that every step we take
toward love
is a step away from fear.
Epiphany is never a spotlight,
never the clear-cut answer
you wish it would be.
It is the flicker of recognition

when you see your word
in the wild—
a street corner protest,
a quiet apology,
the first time you believe
in the possibility of joy
without strings.
Your word becomes a constellation,
guiding you to a place
where you don't just see the light—
you carry it.
Where the star you follow
becomes the one you are.

Meaningful Aging

And Then...

You wake up one morning
and the mirror holds more stories than your eyes can.
Lines etched like maps,
trails of all the roads you've wandered,
and then,
you smile—
because every crease, every shadow,
is a poem your body has written
while you were busy living.

And then,
your hands remember things
they haven't held in years.
The soft weight of a newborn,
the rough edges of a love lost,
the trembling excitement of something just beginning.
You marvel at how steady they still are,
how much they've carried
without complaint.

And then,
you walk a little slower,
but your steps are wiser now.
You know the ground doesn't mind waiting,
the wind still knows your name.
You've learned the art of standing still,
of watching the world spin
without the need to chase it.

And then,
the years fold into you like old friends—
the ones who stayed,
the ones who left without warning.
You sit with them,
share a quiet cup of tea,
knowing that some goodbyes
were meant to last a lifetime,
and then,
you laugh at the tears
you once thought would never stop.

And then,
you find yourself telling stories,
not because you need to be heard,
but because you want to pass the flame,
a little light for someone else's darkness.
Your voice, softer now,
has a way of lingering
like an echo
in the hearts of those who listen.

And then,
you notice the small things
that used to slip by unnoticed—
the way the sun melts into the horizon,
the way the rain smells like earth's forgiveness,
the way love,
even when it's gone,
leaves a warmth that never truly fades.

And then,
you realize aging is not a loss,
but a gathering—
of moments,
of memories,

of everything that mattered
and even the things that didn't.
You gather them close,
and then,
you hold them like treasure
because they are.

And then,
you breathe in the present
as if it's your first breath,
and your last.

Water is Life

The air hums damp,
smelling of moss and earth's heartbeat,
the kind of wet that clings to your skin
and reminds you—
water is life.

Each droplet a prayer,
each root a hymn reaching down
to sip the melody.
The forest breathes in cycles,
and we, small creatures,
are lucky to inhale its song.

Again and Again

I used to think I had to be one thing,
some version of myself that fit into the world
like a key into a lock,
like there was only one way to open the door.
But now I see,
we are always becoming,
shifting with the seasons,
unfolding like the layers of a flower
that doesn't know it's blooming
until its petals catch the sun.

In winter, I thought I had to be still,
that the cold was a sign
to hide what was growing inside me.
But even then,
beneath the frost,
the earth was stretching,
the roots were reaching—
we are never done becoming.

I used to shrink myself to fit in the space
I thought I was given,
bend and twist to be small enough
for other people's comfort.
But becoming is about unlearning that,
about taking up the room
you were always meant to fill
with the full weight of your name,
your voice,
your heartbeat.

It's about letting go of who you thought
you had to be
and becoming the person
you've been all along—
the one who laughs too loud,
cries when the moon is full,
dances when no one's watching,
and says yes to the chaos of growth.

Some days, you'll feel like a storm
raging against yourself,
and other days you'll feel like a quiet field
beneath a soft rain.
Both are true,
both are beautiful,
because being authentically yourself
means embracing every season.

It means knowing you are not static,
that you are the leaves that fall
and the buds that bloom,
the quiet snow
and the rush of spring.
You are all of it—
all the messy, unfinished,
ever-changing parts
that make you whole.

And when you think you've found yourself,
don't be surprised when you start becoming
someone new again,
because that's the secret:
you are allowed to grow,

to shift, to change,

to unfold into whoever you need to be,
again and again,
in every season.

You Matter

Your voice, dear one,
is not a whisper, not a shadow,
but a river longing to break free.
It's the tremor of stars in dark silence,
a flicker in the night
begging to be flame.

Do not wait for the world to grant permission;
the sun does not ask before rising.
Let your voice be like that—
uncontainable, unafraid.
Even if it shakes, even if it stumbles,
let it rise from the cavern of your chest,
soft or fierce, but true.

There is a prayer in the wind,
and it sounds like you

You were born with thunder in your bones,
a language older than words,
woven from the pulse of ancestors
who once knew silence as stone
and shattered it with their cries.

Speak, because the world bends and leans
to listen, because truth wears no mask,
because your voice matters,
even when it feels small as a spark
flickering in the vastness of all things.

Speak, not to change the world,
but to be fully in it—
each word a footprint,
each breath a bridge.
We are not meant to stay quiet,
not when the heart aches like this.

Part Five
Witness

Waiting

Behind each small door,
a whisper: wait.
It's the kind of pause
that doesn't stop time,
but tilts your heart forward,
peeking past the present
into what might come next.
Let's see what's waiting—
a spark of sweetness,
a tiny gift wrapped in paper dreams,
a reminder that joy
can fit in the smallest spaces.
Day by day,
we walk this quiet path
from longing to light,
hands full of little treasures
and hearts fuller still,
knowing the best surprise
is the one we didn't expect.
So let's see what's waiting.
One more day, one more door.
Faith builds its home in the act of opening.

Diagnosis

It starts with a room.
White walls too clean to be holy,
too cold to catch the warmth of a prayer.
And the news comes, not like a storm,
but like the silence after.
A mouthful of emptiness
that swallows even the echoes.

Faith is a funny thing.
It doesn't always wear white robes.
Sometimes it's a cracked voice,
sometimes it's hands clasped tight,
sometimes it's a whispered "stay."
And you sit there, trying to make sense
of the way the air shifts
when hope tries to find a way in.

You think about the mornings
spent tracing the curve of your life,
the days you wore your name
like an answer to a question
no one ever asked.
You remember the times
you loved so big it hurt,
left laughter in rooms
that still hum with your joy
long after you're gone.

Fingerprints.
Little miracles pressed into the world—
not grand, not loud,
but undeniable.
On the backs of those you held,

on the books you left open,
on the doors you forgot to close
because you were always rushing
to something that felt bigger than you.

You tell yourself this isn't the end;
the universe doesn't draw lines
that end in nothing.
Faith whispers it's the part
of the story where shadows
find their source of light.

And if you are to leave,
you will go with open palms,
leaving behind a thousand
tiny marks that say:
"I was here,
and I loved,
and it was enough."

Because fingerprints don't fade
from the lives they've touched.
They stay,
like prayers etched in soft clay,
like hymns in the dark,
like the promise that light
never really leaves.

Beauty in Breaks

In the heart of a home where laughter spills
like sunlight through open windows,
cracked glass in the carpet catches the light,
fractured stories woven into its surface,
each shard a memory,
a moment suspended in time.
And my mind immediately thinks of
feet crunching on the remnants of yesterday,
the echo of joy underfoot,
a symphony of life,
where every step tells a tale,
of children chasing shadows,
of lovers dancing in the kitchen,
the warmth of a shared meal lingering in the air.
Walls adorned with fingerprints,
the artistry of little hands,
painted dreams and crayon wishes,
a testament to the chaos,
the beauty of being alive,
where imperfections are celebrated,
like the laughter that fills the rooms,
bouncing off the cracked glass,
reflecting the light of a life well-lived.
And in this house,
the sound of crunching glass beneath our feet
is not a warning but a reminder,
that even broken things can hold the weight of love,
that life, in all its messy glory,
is a dance of resilience,
where every crack tells a story,
and every laugh is a promise,
that we are here,
together,

in this beautiful, imperfect world.
And so let's find beauty in breaks, in the way we feel
   whole,
Let the worries release,
As we cradle the chaos, and reclaim our souls.

Divine Feminine

In the tapestry of time, the maiden laughs with innocence,
her dreams like blossoms unfurling in spring.
The mother stands strong, a guardian of warmth,
nurturing life, weaving wisdom into each day.
The crone, with a gaze that holds the stars,
shares her tales, ancient echoes of love and loss.
Together, they dance through the seasons of existence,
three faces of the divine, embracing all that is.
In this season, may each of us step forward, with hearts
    wide open,
ready to greet whatever the future holds.
In this dance of ages, may we find our truth,
the embodiment of love in every fleeting moment.

Pay Attention

In the quiet corners of everyday moments,
where sunlight spills like laughter,
and shadows dance with the dust motes,
there lies a magic not meant for belief,
but for noticing,
like the way the wind whispers secrets
to the leaves,
or how the moon blushes
when the stars lean in close,
sharing stories of the universe
that we often forget to listen to.
This year, let us be the witnesses,
the curious souls with eyes wide open,
not searching for miracles in the sky,
but finding them in the mundane,
the way a child finds joy
in the simple act of spinning,
arms outstretched,
as if to embrace the whole world,
in a dizzying twirl of wonder.
Let's notice the way laughter bubbles
up from the depths of our bellies,
how it fills the air like confetti,
and how kindness can be a soft breeze,
a gentle nudge that reminds us
we are all made of stardust,
woven together in this tapestry
of existence,
where every thread is a story,
every moment a spark of whimsy.
So, this year, let us not believe
in magic as a distant dream,
but let it be the pulse of our days,

the shimmer in our conversations,
the unexpected joy in a shared glance,
the way the world unfolds,
not as a puzzle to solve,
but as a wonder to be embraced,
as we walk this path of noticing,
hand in hand with the extraordinary
that resides in the ordinary

Gratitude in Truth

The table stretches long,
laden with stories too heavy to hold.
Behind the harvest's shine,
a shadow of lives uprooted,
names spoken in languages
colonized into silence.

This land,
rich with memory,
asks us to listen,
asks us to honor
not the myth of peace,
but the fight for justice.

Today, let gratitude
be a verb,
a reckoning,
a return.

Let us give thanks
by learning, unlearning,
by standing with those
whose land, whose lineage,
was stolen,
yet still grows strong.

I am Enough

When the world feels heavy,
and the map of your heart is a tangle of roads,
remember,
you are not lost,
you are becoming.
Let the mirror reflect
not just the face,
but the stories etched in your skin,
the laughter that dances in your eyes,
the weight of dreams still waiting
to be born.
Pursue yourself,
like a wildflower reaching for sunlight,
unravel the knots of yesterday,
and breathe in the possibility
of today.
Find joy in the simple,
in the way your heart beats
when you let go of the chase,
when you sit with your own reflection
and whisper,
"I am enough."
Nourish your spirit
with kindness,
wrap your soul in compassion,
and let the healing begin
in the spaces
where you once (maybe even still) felt broken.
Trust that the path will emerge,
not in the frantic search for answers,
but in the stillness of your own becoming,
where happiness expands
like a garden after rain,

and confidence emerges
like the sun each morning and the moon at night.
You are the compass,
the journey,
the destination,
and in each step toward yourself,
the universe will conspire
to lead you home.

Radical Love

It is not soft.
It is a lion's roar in the throat of the smallest bird,
a tree splitting its own roots to feed the starving forest.
Radical love is not gentle;
it is wildfire fierce,
burning through the scripts that told us we were
    unworthy.
It is walking into rooms where you were once
    unwelcome,
hands open, saying:
I will not leave you behind,
even if you cannot yet see the chains you carry.
Radical love is folding rage into forgiveness
without letting go of justice,
it is the revolution born in a mother's hum,
the healing whispered in a stranger's smile.
It is the quiet rebellion of staying soft
when the world tries to harden you,
the relentless choosing of hope
when grief has made its home in your ribs.
Radical love says,
even when it costs everything,
we will keep building,
keep holding,
keep choosing each other.

Story telling

Today, I tell the story.
Because if I don't, who will?
If I don't speak the words that have carried me here,
how will the world know
that I lived,
that I hurt,
that I loved enough to break?

Today, I spill the pieces.
I take them from the corners of my heart
and lay them bare—
the good, the gritty, the things I wish
I could forget but hold onto anyway.
Because stories are bridges,
and we all need a way to cross
from being unknown
to being seen.

Today, I tell the story
of the time I failed,
the time I won,
the time I stood on the edge
and someone's hand pulled me back.
I tell it because maybe someone else
is standing there now,
waiting for the words
that will remind them they're not alone.

Today, I become a witness,
to my own life,
to yours,
to all the stories we think are too small
to matter

but are too big to let go.
And in the telling,
we become real,
solid,
carved into the fabric of the world
so that no one can say
we were never here.
Today, I tell the story,
so you know I lived

Not Perfect

The first time I met him,
he called me child with a voice
like a candle being lit.
Soft, but certain,
like he already knew the rooms of my heart
better than I did.I,
a young minister,
tripping over the weight of my own words,
thinking I had to tear the heavens open
to show God's face.
He,
an old priest,
with hands that had buried more grief than I could
    imagine,
and eyes that had learned
to find resurrection
in the smallest cracks of light.
He said,
God is not the sermon you're writing
at 3 a.m. in a cold church office.
God is the laughter you thought
you'd lost for good,
the bread you forgot to pray over,
but fed the hungry anyway.
When I asked him about tradition,
he laughed.
Tradition is not a box,
he said,
it's a compass.
Let it point, but don't let it trap you.
Even Christ broke rules to heal.
He never cared that my theology was messy,
or that my collar was stitched

from threads of protest and praise.
It's not the vestments that matter,
he told me,
it's the way your voice shakes
when you say "beloved."
Now, when I preach,
I don't try to be perfect.
I try to be open.
Like he taught me.
Like the cracked chalice
still holds the wine.
He reminds me,
every time we meet:
The divine doesn't live
in the things we build.
It lives in the way we
carry each other home

Legacy of Love

I want to love so big
that it outlives me—
stretching beyond my hands,
beyond the edges of my days,
into the spaces I'll never see.
I want my love to flood over,
a river that can't be stopped,
carving its way into the lives
of those I've touched,
those I'll never know.

I want to love so expansively
that the echoes of it
are felt in the soft breath of the future,
woven into the stories
of those who will come long after I've gone,
because love like this doesn't disappear—
it expands,
multiplies,
filling every crack, every gap
we thought was too wide to bridge.

I want to love so deeply
that it becomes the roots
of trees I'll never see grow,
but they'll stand tall one day,
branches full,
because somewhere in the soil
is the love I left behind.

I want to love like this—
so fully,
so endlessly,

that it's a legacy
not written in stone
but in the hearts I've held,
in the kindness I've offered,
in the way I made someone feel
seen, known,
enough.

Because love is the only thing
we leave behind
that doesn't fade—
and I want mine to stretch far,
to whisper to the world
that I was here
and that I loved
so expansively
it became my forever.

Steady

I want to live a life
that feels like something—
not loud, not grand,
but steady as a heartbeat,
carving a quiet place in the world
where kindness grows.

I want to wake each day
with purpose,
not in glory or fame,
but in the small, unspoken things:
the hands I've held,
the burdens I've shared,
the laughter I've sparked
in rooms filled with shadows.

I want to leave behind
a trail of moments
where love was louder than fear,
where I gave more than I took,
where the world, even just a little,
felt softer because I was here.

I want to live a life
worthy of being remembered,
not for how bright I shone,
but for the warmth I left
in the hearts of those who needed it most.

In the Air

Up here, the earth becomes
a quilt someone forgot to finish—
fields stitched in uneven squares,
rivers threading silver through the seams,
cities dotting the fabric like stray buttons.
From this height,
the highways stop roaring,
the houses stop shouting,
the inbox stops buzzing in my skull.

I can see everything
but touch nothing.
And it feels like relief—
like someone hit pause
on the chaos below.

From this distance,
there are no overdue notices,
no cracked phone screens,
no dishes balancing like bad decisions
in the sink.
There is only the horizon
stacked in colors too soft for worry:
gold bleeding into rose,
a blue so tender it forgets
to be sky.

The plane bumps,
and my stomach tumbles,
a reminder that I am still small,
still human, still carried
by something much larger than myself.
Gravity holds its hands out beneath me,

just in case.

Perspective is not found,
it is borrowed—
a gift from the altitude.
Down there, I am an ant
shouldering the world.
Up here, I am only a speck
drifting through air
and possibility.

The fields blur into a mosaic.
The rivers become veins,
pulsing life into land.
I think of how tiny my problems must look
from this high up,
how maybe, just maybe,
they too are part of the pattern.

The plane begins its descent,
clouds closing over the view
like a curtain.
Soon, I'll be back in the noise,
the scramble,
the ordinary everything.
But for now, I carry this quiet:
a pocket-sized horizon,
a quilt stitched with distance,
a promise that not every moment
has to feel so impossibly heavy.

Defiant Joy

Joy doesn't whisper—
it roars like the ocean,
like thunder shaking the sky.
It is a fistful of wildflowers
breaking through the cracks
in the pavement of despair.
Defiant joy grows anyway,
screams anyway,
dances on bruised feet,
laughing through tears
because it knows:
to resist is to survive,
to celebrate is to fight.
It's a protest song at dawn,
a spark that lights the coldest dark.
Joy, unapologetic,
is the anthem of the undefeated,
the hymn of the unbroken.

Sacred Pause

Death is a pause,
a breath caught in the throat of time,
a sacred silence
that lingers between heartbeats,
reminding us that even endings
hold grace.

We stand at the edge,
bearing witness to the stillness,
the quiet unraveling of one life's thread,
and though we feel the weight
of that pause,
the world hums onward,
a soft and steady rhythm
that does not stop for sorrow.

Flowers bloom,
stars rise and fall,
and somewhere, a child laughs
without knowing
the earth beneath their feet
has shifted.

In the quiet after the storm,
we remember—
death is not an ending,
but a part of the dance.
A beat in the song
we all belong to,
a sacred rhythm we will one day join,
when the pause comes for us.

And the world will go on.

It always does.
But the space we leave behind
will echo with the lives we've touched,
a gentle ripple
in the endless current.

Morning

Morning arrives cloaked,
a shroud of fog rising from the water,
ghosts escaping the lake's quiet mouth.
It drapes the trees in mystery,
softens the edges of the world
until nothing feels sharp enough to hurt.

For a moment, the earth exhales magic.
The kind that makes you stop mid-thought,
mid-breath, mid-life,
to wonder if change always begins this softly—
a veil lifting, a whisper of what's to come.

The fog doesn't linger.
It never does.
It unravels like thread,
dispersing into daylight,
a magician's sleight of hand
leaving nothing but clarity.
And yet, for those fleeting moments,
it transforms the ordinary into the sacred,
the seen into the hidden,
the fixed into the fluid.

Change, it seems,
isn't the sudden snap we fear,
but the slow unmaking of what was,
the gentle breath of possibility
rolling in waves we don't always notice
until we're knee-deep in its beauty.

Watch it rise,
watch it fade,
watch the world beneath it emerge anew—
not better, not worse,
just another version of itself,
another chapter in a story
we never stop writing.

We are no different.
We rise from ourselves
and return again,
dissolving what we thought we'd always be
to make space for what we could become.
The lake keeps no record of the fog;
it holds the stillness,
waits for the next unveiling.

We Give Thanks

We give thanks for the Wampanoag,
who met the Mayflower's shore.
For the Cherokee, forced to walk
trails of sorrow, yet still singing.
For the Lakota, who hold the Black Hills sacred,
though treaties were broken like brittle promises.

We remember the Diné,
whose sheep and songs shape the desert.
The Coast Salish, who know the language of salmon.
The Ojibwe, who listen as birch trees whisper wisdom.

Each name a heartbeat,
Shoshone, Seminole, Choctaw,
Nez Perce, Pueblo, Mohican—
their histories woven into the soil.

This land is not ours to own,
but to steward in their honor.
Let our thanks be a call to repair,
to acknowledge, to act,
until every name is spoken with reverence,
until every life is cherished whole.

Somatics

In the dim light of the room,
where whispers of lavender linger,
hands become the language of healing,
tracing the map of a body
that has carried the weight of unspoken stories.
Fingers dance like soft rain,
each touch a gentle reminder
that the skin remembers,
that muscles hold the echoes
of laughter turned to silence,
of joy pressed into corners
where shadows still linger.
Breath deepens, a tide rising,
as the body learns to trust,
to unravel the knots of yesterday,
to release the grip of time,
each exhale a surrender,
each inhale a reclamation.
In this sacred space,
the heart beats louder,
a drum calling back lost parts,
as tension melts like winter's frost,
and the soul whispers,
"I am here, I am safe,
I am more than the sum of my scars."
With every stroke,
the past slips away,
like water through fingers,
and in the stillness,
the body remembers how to be whole,
how to bloom in the warmth of presence,
how to rise anew,

a phoenix wrapped in tender hands,
ready to embrace the light.

Christmas Adventure

On a chill Christmas morning,
the world breathes softly,
frost painting the windows,
we layer up, hearts eager,
and set out on a drive,
the road unwinding like a ribbon,
leading us to a gathering,
where thirty plus souls collide,
laughter spilling over,
hugs wrapping us in warmth,
chaos and love intertwining,
stories shared like gifts,
the spirit of the season alive.
As dusk settles,
the air cools,
and we find solace in the quiet,
the drive home a gentle embrace,
the glow of headlights guiding us,
through the stillness,
reflecting on the joy,
the laughter echoing softly,
a chill Christmas evening,
woven together in memory.

Throw Back

In the folds of my mind,
laughter lingers like sunlight,
I wander through this maze of innocence,
chasing shadows of forgotten days.
Time dances lightly,
as I gather these fragments,
a treasure chest of joy and wonder.
I hear their whispers,
the echoes of a simpler heart,
and I smile, knowing they live on,
in the depths of my soul, forever young.

The Bigger Picture

We are small.
We are specks of light in a universe
too vast to name.
But we are here,
and that is the whole point—
to be here.
To breathe through the chaos
and feel the pulse of every moment
inside our chest.

The bigger picture is not about us,
but we are a part of it,
woven into its fabric like threads of fire,
like roots in the earth.
We rise, we fall, we bloom, we break—
but always together,
always in the same garden
where the soil remembers
every seed,
every hand that's ever tried to plant hope
even when it felt impossible.

There's right-sizing in this,
the humbling truth
that our stories matter
but they're not the only ones.
We are not the whole sky,
but a constellation within it,
our light meaningful
because it joins with others,
because it guides the way.

To thrive is to know

that survival is collective.
It's the hands we hold,
the shoulders we lean on
when the weight of the world
feels too much to carry alone.

And yes, death comes,
fear chokes us some nights,
and the news screams louder than hope,
but even in the darkest corners,
there is a heartbeat,
a rhythm that says we belong
to something bigger,
something ancient,
something that sings when we cannot.

The bigger picture is the community we build,
the voices that rise when ours crack,
the arms that catch us when we fall
and lift us back into the light,
again and again.

Because none of this is about standing alone.
It's about standing together,
about knowing that in every season—
in every moment of healing,
chaos,
renewal—
we are part of a symphony,
and it is louder,
it is stronger,
it is more beautiful
than anything we could ever be
on our own.

Beginnings

The year exhales like a candle,
a flicker, then stillness.
It is the sound of a door closing,
the soft scrape of snow
against the soles of your shoes.
You measure the months
in almosts and agains,
in the weight of what you carried
and the grace of what let you go.
There is no countdown for healing,
no ball that drops to say
you are new.
But still, the clock turns.
Still, you step forward,
into whatever waits,
into whatever comes next—
a whisper, a roar,
a beginning.

Reader's Reflections

These are your pages. They're for you to jot down a thought, a feeling, or even your own poem. Don't overthink it. This isn't about creating something perfect; it's about showing up for yourself. Just as the poems invite you to pause and reflect, these blank spaces ask you to join the conversation.